Cry of Strange Dreams

Stories and Poems of Spain

Cry of Strange Dreams

Stories and Poems of Spain

Dolores de Leon

≡⌂≡

Ashland Hills Press

Short stories in this volume were originally published in literary journals, as follows:
"Mulo" - Published in the journal, *Left Curve*, Spring, 2007
"Fingers" - Published in *Zahir*, Spring, 2008
"Evil Eye" - Published in *River's Edge*, Spring, 2008
"Miracle Child" - Published in *Madison Review*, Fall, 2007
"Deception" - Published in *Amoskeag*, Spring, 2007,
           and *Arnazella*, May, 2007
"Ring" - Published in *Thereby Hangs a Tail*, April, 2007

Cover and book design by Nancy Parker

Front cover photo and interior section graphic images
by Larry A. Dubbs.

ISBN 978-0-9642272-7-9

Library of Congress Control Number: 2014936996

Published by Ashland Hills Press, P.O. Box 992, Ashland, OR 97520
Phone 541-951-1129

Author's web site: www.DoloresdeLeon.com

First Edition.

Printed in the United States of America.

Matador

The sun bends
        time
Over the arena
Blood-puddled

El Yiyo is alone
Back arched
In an arrogant cliché
His hands hold
The red cloth hiding
        steel

His quick feet
Step in to kill the
            black bull
But a snap of its
            massive head

Cry of strange dreams

And El Yiyo is
        thrown
White horns
Tear at the spilled
        body
That rolls in the sand
Caught in the cape
        ~
El Yiyo is
            dead
At twenty-one
Mouth contorted
Eyes astonished

As if
He never   before
Experienced
            death.

Table of Contents

Table of Contents

Introduction to Spain:

Ring

Pepino, battered by the heat, walked quickly through the streets of Sevilla; he looked neither left nor right. He knew a Gypsy's soul resides in his shadow, and noon, a dead moment in time, was reason enough to hurry. But an even greater reason was the fear he was carrying in his back pocket.

~

The sun directly overhead struck sharp, canceling all shade. Not even the ancient buildings, their facades carved and filigreed by the Moors, nor the recent ones—plain, ugly—had shadows.

On the second floor of one of the grimy, straight-up-and-straight-down buildings in Pepino's barrio, rarely visited by tourists, was the flat where he and his wife Pastora and their baby Miguel Antonio lived.

The sun seeped into Pastora's kitchen. As she worked scrubbing the scarred, scraped wooden counter, the dented pots and blackened pans, the bent forks and spoons, she thought about the dark places, the slits, cracks and holes where the Evil One dwells.

She asked herself if she had plugged every drain in the sinks, shower and tub after they had been used. Was there a chipped mirror anywhere in the flat? The cracks in the windows. Had she taped all of them? Was there a mouse hole she had missed?

She wondered which was more dangerous: the secret places of the Evil One, never known until the damage was done, or a Gypsy caught outside at noon with no shadow to shelter his soul?

Both were happening to Pepino. But neither was the worst. Having to deal with Inocencio—that was the worst.

Pastora shuddered.

~

Making his way rapidly, keeping close to the buildings, Pepino was a small unimportant figure relative to any Spaniard. But he was not concerned with them, with one notable exception: Inocencio, who lived conveniently close to the river. More than one body found floating face down had been his doing.

He was legend in Sevilla. Moving through the underbelly of the city, the drug dealers, the petty crooks, the not-so-petty crooks, knowing everyone and their secret terrors, Inocencio spread his web, worked one connection against another, and never got caught, not by the police, certainly. Nor, more remarkably, by his own kind.

For Pepino, however, he was simply a way to quick money. There was that first time when Pepino found the exceptionally large pearl in an oyster; there was a second time when a dirty little bag of stolen jewels was left in his keeping. These had gotten him easy cash.

But the third time he went to Inocencio, Pepino put himself in the worst possible position: having nothing to exchange, he asked for a straight-out loan.

Pepino paid no attention to the due date on the loan.

Money was love to Pepino. Once in his hands, the money was his and no one else's, not the bar's that had given him credit, not the green grocer's nor the fishmonger's nor the landlord's. Nor Inocencio's.

Not until he got the call from Inocencio whose words, rapid, soft-spoken, suggesting crushed and broken bones and missing fingers, turned Pepino's face ashen white and sent him scurrying through his flat, digging in coat pockets and under cushions for money.

Finding not nearly enough, Pepino spent a sleepless night imagining one scheme after another for getting out of Inocencio's grasp, fully aware none of them would work.

It was the very next morning, however, that he found the ring wedged in a crack in the sidewalk in front of his building. Digging it out, he turned it over and over in his hands. A simple gold band set with one large yellow gem, it gave off a compelling light. Even in its dirtied, trampled condition, Pepino couldn't keep his eyes off of it.

He wiped it clean, tried it on one finger, took it off, tried it on another finger, bit on it, rubbed it between his palms. The longer he held it, the more he wanted it. Deciding it was his and no one else's, he took it home and showed it to his brother Aurelio who was living with Pastora and Pepino for an indeterminate, unwelcome length of stay.

"It's a piece of junk," Aurelio said.

"Aurelio, you wouldn't know a jewel if it bit you," Pepino replied.

Then he showed the ring to Pastora in her kitchen. "I can sell it and make enough to pay off Inocencio and have money left over," he chortled.

Pastora, however, absorbed in the devious ways of the Evil One, took one look and said, "It's round, Pepino!"

"Of course it's round."

"And it has a hole, Pepino. A hole!"

"Don't be an idiot, Pastora. All rings have holes. How else can you get them on a finger?"

"Pepino, the Evil One can get in!"

"Pastora, don't be an idiot," Pepino repeated.

But that night, the rooms of the flat inexplicably shifted. What was in one place was now in another. Pastora's kitchen was out on the balcony, and Pepino, half asleep, killed her best fern when he peed on it because it was where the bathroom should have been. Most frightening, however, was when baby Miguel Antonio cried. For a few panicky moments he could not be found; he was not where the cries were coming from.

By morning Pepino was rattled. When Pastora told him the Evil One had come through the ring and Pepino should take it at once to Inocencio, he did not argue with her.

~

With its bright white buildings trimmed in yellow, its plazas, orange trees, outdoor cafes, horse-drawn carriages, the Barrio Santa Cruz is a haven for tourists. They never guess that beneath their feet is a second city, an ancient rats maze of interlacing tunnels scooped out by the Moors in the eighth century. Dark and circuitous, it was a secret way for the caliphate to cross old Sevilla quickly, thereby avoiding the sun and the swarming foot traffic on the sidewalks above.

Pepino, as a boy living on the streets, stealing food, dodging the Guardias, had known about the tunnels. As an adult, the tunnels were no more mysterious to him than the lines on his hands.

~

Leaving behind his own barrio, Pepino weaseled his way through the winding streets of the Barrio Santa Cruz, watchful for the entrance to the tunnels. Slipping between two old buildings, he ducked through a narrow doorway and went quickly down an ancient stairway of stone steps leading to the tunnels.

Once in the tunnels, he began rabbit-running, knowing where to turn when there was a choice, knowing which ones were dead-ends but with a slit he could squeeze through, knowing exactly the tunnel that would come out closest to Inocencio's apartment building.

Normally Pepino could have run the maze without thinking. But this time he had the sensation of something not quite right. Dimly lit at best, were the tunnels darker than usual? His shoulders were brushing the walls. Were the tunnels narrower? And the stones under his feet. Were they rougher? Once, twice, he almost stumbled.

Then his foot caught on a protruding stone and he fell hard.

For a moment he was stunned, unable to think. Getting up, he felt he was in a different place than he had been before. He dismissed the idea, putting it down to the fall jarring his senses.

Dusting himself off, he started to run again. But the tunnels darkened and narrowed even as he ran through them. Terror became Pepino's mind. Choking for air, he stopped and flattened himself up against a wall. Digging his fingers into the hard surface, he inched slowly along.

Then abruptly there were no more walls. There was no tunnel; there was nothing. He was standing in blackness on a bit of ground no bigger than his own two feet.

Even so, Pepino, shivering, nauseated, had enough sense to know what he must do. He had known all along: the ring was deadly. He pulled it out of his back pocket and dropped it at his feet.

The ring glowed. Pepino wanted to pick it up again, hold it, warm it in his hands. Instead, he took the risk of his life: he moved his right heel backwards just an inch, half-expecting there would be nothing underneath it. But the ground *was* there and so were the tunnels. It was his world again—and familiar.

He turned around and ran.

~

Out of the tunnels and up on the street, Pepino grasped at the sunlight with his eyes. He was happy, for a moment, until he remembered that, without the ring, he was in as bad a predicament as before.

He wanted to go away. But go away *where?* If he went home, he faced the wrath of Inocencio. If he went forward, he faced the wrath of Inocencio.

Numb, he began weaving through the crowds of Spaniards hurrying along in the opposite direction. Oblivious to their excited chatter, he didn't ask himself why they were out at siesta hour.

Hesitantly, he entered Inocencio's building.

The deep, dark shade of its tiled entranceway should have been soothing to Pepino, but he was alone and afraid. He buzzed and hoped there would be no response. But a moment later the front door opened silently.

As he made his way up the stairs, his hands left sweat marks on the banister; they shook as he knocked at the door.

It was Inocencio's woman who answered the door. Her face drawn and white, she didn't speak for a moment. But when she did, she simply said, "It's all over. The crowds at the river. That body they found. It was Inocencio."

I. VILLAGES

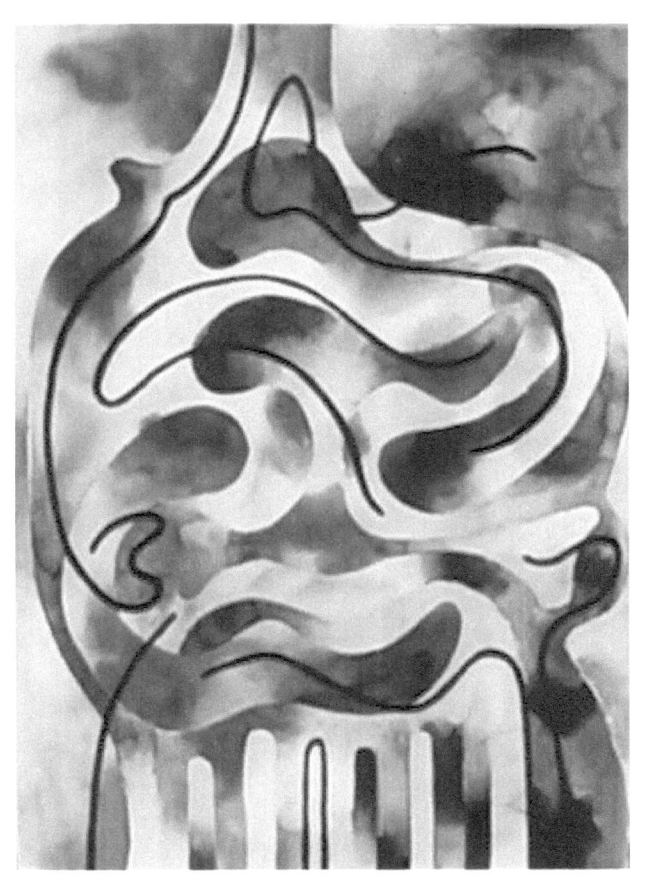

Mulo

Among the Gypsies of southern Spain, the Mulo *is an avenging spirit sent forth by the recently deceased. A middle finger, or replica of one, placed in front of the grave is the only way a* Mulo *can be stopped from rising.*

~

In Sevilla, at one minute after midnight, Aurelio heard the ravens. He knew, for what he had done, that his mother had sent them. And he knew, for a certainty, her *Mulo* was right behind them.

Aurelio squeezed into the narrow crack between two buildings. He could hear the ravens beating their wings against the roofs.

There was no light in the crack; he moved through it by feeling along with his fingers. As soon as they were touched by cool air, he pulled himself out from between the buildings. He was at the river—safe for the moment—a *Mulo* wouldn't go near water.

~

Ana Maria speaks*: I'm nine years old and getting older. It was two weeks ago my Grandma died. The night before Grandma died, Grandpa sang to her about the sun 'cause she was cold. She was always cold. But she never died from it before. My mama says she died 'cause my Uncle Aurelio left the clan and made a hole for the Evil One to get in.*

Uncle Aurelio came back to Spain for Grandma's funeral but he was five days late. He's staying with my Uncle Pepino and Aunt Pastora in Sevilla. He sits on the edge of the bed all day playing his guitar. When he takes it out of the case, he says, "Hello, Sweet baby." And when he puts it away he says, "Later baby."

No one says what's the matter with Uncle Aurelio. No one says why he runs down the middle of the street at night crying. I asked my mama. And she kissed the top of my head and said it was 'cause Uncle Aurelio was no more. "No more, Mama?"

"No more, Ana. He left and you can't leave. Gypsies can't leave."

But I dream of leaving Spain and going to America. My mama says I have nothing in that place. What can they teach you she says, when you can already read the signs.

It's true. When my baby sister died, I knew 'cause the snakes in the patio were still. And I can hear people's dreams when they're awake. I can hear my Uncle Aurelio's day dreams. My Grandma's death crawls across his dreams like worms on a tablecloth.

Uncle Aurelio said to me at Grandpa's house, "Have you ever seen snow, Ana?"

"No, Uncle."

"Have you ever seen an elephant?"

"No, Uncle."

"Ana, you visit me when I go back to America, and I promise I will show you a canyon as big as all Andalucia."

But my mama says I can't go 'cause Uncle Aurelio killed Grandma.

~

Aurelio walked along the riverbank. He kicked at the damp earth until he found a small piece of wood. Kneeling, he whittled at it with his pocket knife, holding it up now and then and comparing it to his own middle finger. Then he put the little piece of wood in his pocket, walked up to the boulevard and hailed a cab. "The cemetery," he said to the driver.

"The cemetery? At night?"

"Just take me there."

"You're nuts. Or a Gypsy. *Madre de Dios!* You're a Gypsy! *Hombre,* I'm not giving any free rides."

"I've got the money."

"Then you're not from around here. Where you from?"

"You've got a big mouth."

"I'm just curious. I know everybody in Sevilla. So where you from?"

"California. But I was born here."

"America? *Madre de Dios.* A Gypsy in America!"

"Just drive."

~

Aurelio climbed the wall of the cemetery. He lit a match to read

18

each gravestone. With his last match he found his mother's. Standing back, he called out, "Magdalena Carlota Ayala y Mendoza, hear me."

The earth shook under him.

"Thank you, Mama, for hearing me. But Mama, you can't do this. Call back your *Mulo*. It wants to kill me. I have the wooden finger. I'll put it on your grave and your *Mulo* will be left outside and will die. Mama, talk to me, tell me you'll call off your *Mulo*."

But the earth under his feet was silent, though the sky wasn't. Aurelio could hear the ravens approaching. He stooped in front of the gravestone and started digging a little trough. Loose dirt came up through his fingers; he felt the soft, moving flesh of a worm. Shuddering, he took the wooden finger from his pocket and placed it in the trough.

The ground trembled. "Mama," he said, "don't cry. I'm sorry. I really am. But I warned you."

~

The pain woke Aurelio up. "You an angel?" he asked the figure standing over him.

The angel, unshaven and wearing a wrinkled gray uniform, the cuffs hanging down over his dirty finger nails, kicked the sole of Aurelio's foot again. "You lousy Gypsy. Up! Out of here!"

Aurelio, ignoring the angel, got to his hands and knees and searched the dirt in front of the gravestone until he found the wooden finger. "It worked," he murmured, and then, "I'm sorry, Mama."

"You're talking to the dirt," the angel said.

"Mama," Aurelio went on, "now you can't send another *Mulo*. You can't kill me anymore."

"You dead?" asked the angel.

Aurelio stood up and brushed himself off. "I thought I was. I guess I'm not."

~

Ana Maria speaks: *Uncle Aurelio told everybody that he'd stopped Grandma's* Mulo. *But it isn't good to stop a* Mulo.

My mama wasn't happy about it. She called my aunt Constancia.

Aunt Constancia always knows what to say to make Mama feel worse. She said that now Grandma's Mulo *was outside her grave, Grandma would never be able to go to Glory. And Mama cried.*

The next morning Uncle Aurelio said he was going back to California early 'cause no one understands him in Spain. I asked my mama again if I could go with him. She said no again, but then she said I could go stay a while with my Uncle Pepino and Aunt Pastora in their flat.

~

Aurelio walked along the boulevard above the river to the airline office.

The woman in the blue uniform in front of the computer didn't look up. Aurelio watched her lips move. He asked her to repeat it. It didn't get any better: "Sir, because of the special one-time low fare, we can't exchange your ticket or give you a refund. You do understand."

Aurelio didn't understand. He banged on the counter with both fists. He yelled, "What the hell do you *mean*?"

And he would have banged more and yelled more, but he felt someone behind him. Aurelio turned around. The security guard stood over him with one hand on his revolver. Breathing short, quick breaths down on Aurelio's face, he spoke quietly, but persuasively.

At the bar across the street, Aurelio put his last *duros* on the counter and ordered a beer. He sat and took stock of his assets. He didn't have any. Well, maybe one. Her name was Lourdes.

Over his cold beer, he thought about her. He didn't know where to find her. He didn't even know her last name. She had said she lived near a convent. There were two in Sevilla. Aurelio finished his beer and headed for the nearest one.

In the street, he spoke to the first nun he saw. From her he got Lourdes's address, her last name, when she was home, and the exact hours her husband worked.

A half-hour later, Aurelio lay in flower-blooming sheets sprinkled with sweet perfume. Lourdes had her big legs wrapped around him while she held his face between her blimp breasts with one hand and played with his black curls with the other.

Aurelio, feeling himself suffocating, pulled back his head and told Lourdes she was beautiful.

Lourdes smiled all her gold fillings at him. "My little Gypsy Love," she said, "your Lourdes is going to buy you a shirt."

Aurelio told her he loved her.

"You need a suit, too, *mi amor*."

He told her he canceled his flight to California just so he could be with her.

Lourdes didn't reply. She reached a long, fleshy arm to the drawer of the night table, took out a roll of bills, and dropped it in Aurelio's shoe.

That afternoon, in a pink suit, pink shirt and pink suede shoes, Aurelio went back to the airline office and bought a ticket for California.

~

Ana Maria speaks: *Lourdes comes to visit Uncle Aurelio every day. Uncle Pepino likes to open the door for her 'cause his nose comes right up to her breasts. They're big and they bounce. Especially when she runs down the hall to Uncle Aurelio's room singing* Aurelio, Aurelio. Your lady of miracles is coming for you.

Uncle Aurelio says he's going back to California in a week. But when I say I want to go with him, he only gets this funny look on his face and says, "Huh?" He doesn't remember he ever asked me to California.

I don't cry. I just go into my Aunt Pastora's room. I love my Aunt Pastora. She's fat and eats all the time. She lets me come in bed with her in the mornings and share her breakfast. This morning she saw I was upset; she thought it was over Grandma dying. But that wasn't it at all. I was mad at Uncle Aurelio and wanted to get even.

Aunt Pastora said we should go put flowers on Grandma's grave. So we got all dressed up. Aunt Pastora wore her red dress with the big purple polka-dots and she carried a shopping bag full of food in case she got hungry.

By the time we got to the cemetery, her feet were so swollen we had to sit down on Grandma's grave. That's when I saw the little piece of wood in front of her gravestone. I asked Aunt Pastora what it was. She said it was a wooden finger and just leave it alone 'cause the Evil One had put it there. But I was thinking it was Uncle Aurelio. So while she was looking through the shopping bag for something to eat, I picked up the wooden finger and put it in my pocket. I shouldn't have done that—I knew what would happen.

~

That night, Aurelio felt the presence of his mother in his sleep, smelled her scent of olive oil and roses, heard her whispery words become an angry hiss: "Aurelio, you owe me! I've done everything for you. I've lied and cheated and stolen for you. You never should have left Spain. And don't think I'll ever take you back. No, not even me!"

Just before dawn, Aurelio's mother turned sideways in her grave and pulled another *Mulo* from her anus. It rose up through the coffin, through the black soil into the sky, and began looking for Aurelio.

21

~

Ana Maria speaks: *Uncle Aurelio has heard the ravens again. He wanted to go right back to California. But his flight isn't for a week. So he went in the bathroom and sat on the toilet and let the water run in the tub to keep away the* Mulo.

And he'd still be sitting there, but Señora Ortega came up and said Lourdes's husband had a knife and was down in the plaza asking everyone where Uncle Aurelio lived.

Well, Uncle Aurelio decided he'd be safer at the cemetery. So he got dressed up in his pink suit and went in the kitchen and got out Aunt Pastora's old wooden spoon and carved a new finger to put in front of Grandma's grave. But his hands were shaking so much, he cut his finger and it bled all over his pink suit.

~

In the taxi, Aurelio could hear the ravens, and the high, thin whistle of the *Mulo* as it followed him to the cemetery. Aurelio, his left middle finger throbbing under the bandages, watched through the window as the *Mulo's* sickly yellow-green film began to smear across the moon. He smelled the fetid odor of the miasma that could engulf him and suck out his life.

At the cemetery, Aurelio walked quickly to his mother's grave. "Mama," he said, "I have another wooden finger. I will use it, Mama. I will. I, huh, Mama? My own finger? I cut it. You say you want to see it? Then Mama, call off your *Mulo*."

The whistling stopped.

Aurelio began unwinding the gauze. He counted the layers out loud: "*Two* layers," he said. "Remember, Mama, when I was two? The Guardias smashing our wagon? You hiding with me in the burned-out trunk of a tree? *Three* layers, Mama—you bought me my first guitar. Remember, Mama? *Five* layers—I started lessons on that half-size guitar. You gave me a sweet if I paid attention. *Eight* layers—you gave me *pesetas* for every hour I practiced. *Ten* layers, Mama, you had a guitar made for me. Mama, *fourteen* layers—do you remember? I played for the agents. You told me what contracts to accept."

As he undid the last layer of gauze, Aurelio said, "*Sixteen*, Mama. My first big solo concert. You bought me a pink suit."

Then Aurelio held up the swollen purple finger.

A shiver went through him. Even as he was watching, the bleeding

22

slit was moving towards the base of his finger.

Aurelio let out a cry, "Mama, what are you doing! Mama, you can't do this to me!"

The earth trembled under his feet; the lessening moon grew even darker, and the whistling began again.

"Mama, Mama. What are you asking? If I give you what you want, I'll never play the guitar again!"

Aurelio, weeping, fell to his knees. "All right, Mama. All right. I do want you back. I do. I hear you."

Then placing his left hand in front of the gravestone, he stretched out his middle finger. Taking out his pocket knife, he opened the largest blade with his right hand.

Aurelio looked up. The moon was clear. The whistling had stopped. Aurelio was calm.

Epilogue

Ana Maria speaks: *It's my fault Uncle Aurelio cut off his finger. But I don't feel too bad 'cause he's carried off the bad Fate for the whole clan.*

But then this morning Aunt Pastora bought some flowers and asked me to go to the cemetery with her. I didn't want to go 'cause I didn't want to see the finger. But when we got to Grandma's gravestone there wasn't much to see. The finger was all wrinkled and black.

I asked Aunt Pastora if we should bury it. She said leave it alone. But I took some petals and knelt down to cover it up.

That's when I saw the fingernail. It was still growing, all pink and long, just like when Uncle Aurelio used to play the guitar.

Spanish Villages

There is a Spaniard today, who wants
to live and is starting to live,
between one Spain dying
and another Spain yawning.
        —Antonio Machado

Leave me alone to walk
        these streets
Drag my fingers on their
        chalk facades
Peer through
Silent sunken windows

At the women
Picking saffron threads
From purple flowers
As Jesus carries
                a cross
Up and down the stairs

Not careless of my vision
I would let old Spain
        be
Let it have a distinct
        dark color
Beneath its seamless
        white skin

I ask only
The humbleness of these
        villages

That their white walls
Be not watered down
Nor washed away.

Old Islam

A jagged man plods a narrow holy
                    street
His shadow bends a corner and winds
                    uphill

                    ~

Deeply pitted, worn
This is a small village
Its unceasing houses joined one to
                    another
Swarm upwards to an Arabic castle

These villages yield to my touch
I feel the rough walls against
            my shoulders
Run my hands over the porous
                    ruts

The black garbed people sing to me
As I walk and watch them
Appear and disappear

                    ~

Siesta hours
White hot siesta hours
Heavy bright sun
Soothes all ambition
Drives it away for the sake
                    of a few olives
                        on a plate.

Northern Spain: Burgos

The steeples of its cathedral
           cut the air
Chisel the sky with baubles
Repeat the popping explosions
           of small form

Burgos
An insular self-satisfied city
           with petty pleasures
None of the dirty lavish South
And its effusive entangled wash
           of being

Nor the guitar
Slim music
Hidden in the blood stream

Burgos
Life regulated, correct
Couples amble without questions
None of the hungry thievery of the
           South
With its indulgence in art

Burgos
One wonders
When and where the limits
           unwind

Its cathedral is a stone thrown at
           the sky.

Sevilla

I remember the city I could hold
        in one hand
My fingertips could span its streets
Grasp the dappled shadows
On fifteenth-century walls no higher
        than my head

In hidden patios with cool tile walls
I could sit with ferns up to
        my waist
Trace their tendrils with my fingers

Morning markets
I felt the round-bodied weight
        of the women
As they sifted by me
Watched their hands test the contour
        of fresh eggs
           the flesh of fish

In plazas only twenty footfalls to
        the other side
I sat close to the guitarists
Watched their hands play music
Meant to be heard by just a few

At night in slim spaces in small bars
I saw the men and women dance the
        Sevillanas
Criss-cross and caress each other
        but only with
           their fingertips

        ~

Sevilla
Built to mankind's
        measurements
No high-rise ice nor steel nor glass
        darkens its streets.

Córdoba

In my slurring morning mind
Dreams and memories merge
I am not where I thought
But rather in an old city:

Córdoba takes the walker
            inward
Cloistered
Quiet as a cloak floating
            on water
Its canopies of white muslin
Billow over alleyways
Thin as threads
Leading to the Mosque

                ~

Once
The muezzin's call opened every
                morning
Men in thick white robes weaved
                beneath
The red and white striped archways
Before they curled their bodies
            to the floor

Light still slips between these
                columns
Illumines the four hundred
                arches
Rising fresh
In soundless exultation

And I?
I also weave beneath
Those curves of color
Hold their silent joy within
Until my body is itself
                the rising light
The sense of Beautiful.

Three Cities:

1. Segovia

A seagull wheels above me
I assume his form
Broad wings propelling
        me
To warmer winds

I descend slowly
Past red tile roofs
Past the lyric arches of
        an aqueduct
Spread wide my webbed feet
Land on cobblestones
Fold my wings—and wait

Terra cotta houses
Are carved in *mudéjar* rosettes
The air is thick with garlic
        and hot olive oil
An old woman dressed in black
        sits in a window
Talks in slurred Castilian
        to her cat

Standing in the sun
I take it all in
It goes down so easily
Like a long-awaited drink of water.

2. Ronda

Reina de Los Cielos
Where the bridge ends the old city begins
                    it is white
In crevices where shadows ought to be--white
Around corners where darkness should define the
                    edges—white

In one-room markets close with sausages
The braids of garlic hang like hair
Women with old apple faces talk and laugh
The hidden Christ behind their eyes
Reminds them where they're living:
Ronda—Queen of Heaven—ledge city

At dusk at Ronda's edge
The black bulls
Cross the valley floor far below

Thin wavering lines behind
                    low rock walls
Their horns are
White crescents in the pallid night.

3. Consuegra

In the grit of a dry afternoon
Empty streets are left to cool alone
There is no movement but the heat
I climb a hill and view
A distant plain
A stretch of red
A sea
        gone hard

After siesta
The old men of Consuegra sit
Watch the windmills of their inner eye
The shadow of Don Quixote caught in time
Moving like a spear across
                    the bleeding plain

Where plateaus rise
While crenellated walls
Of castles fall in slow
        motion
Waiting centuries to crumble

      ~

I've seen the fountains of Sevilla
The azure pools and roses of Granada
The orange gardens of old Córdoba
But the lonely barren plain
I love much more

After siesta I stand
Wait for it to
        awaken
But it only buzzes its name—*La Mancha.*

Santiago De Compostela

The old town, as well as the Cathedral
of Santiago de Compostela, was built
in the eleventh century over the grave
of St. James.

After Santander—
The blue coast and hanging bridge
Lift of peaks and curves
Roads around weed and thistle
A country as medieval
As Galicia allows—
Comes Santiago

The Old City

A blind man
Wondering where his
         world went
Walks his fingers
Along Santiago's ancient walls
Of faded stones
With clusters of purple
       flowers
Growing through their
       crevices

I remember the woven
       winding
Streets
Warmed by years of walking
Its restaurants built into
       dark stone
Its windows alive with the
       wet prevalence
Of slippery sliding
         pink-eyed fish
Reminding us of the early
       pilgrimages
Their illusive circumstance
       of travel:

Old maps failing them
Pilgrims poked and probed
The resistant ground
The bristle of desolate paths
      and hard hills
(Add thievery, murder, mayhem)

Nevertheless
They came to Compostela
With the conviction of
        the forgiven
To worship at the bones
    of divinity

The Cathedral

The Word in stone
Stays
Though its dark golden eye
Is a storm of unresolved
     inquest
That no one can explain
    away

Near its walls
The thin wheeling wail
Of an unseen bagpipe
Ricochets off
The gangly spires
As an exuberance of bells
Announces Mass

Inside
Gilded angels talk
    in soft voices
The feet of starry Virgins
Clutch at crescent
    moons

~

Stony faces of
Devils and demons
Poke through walls
At pilgrims placing
      hands on a statue

~

From mausoleum
To cloisters
To museum
Is nine flights up
I trudged the steps
      all of them
But felt no closer to
      God.

Granada

The greatest sadness is to be blind in Granada.
—Spanish proverb

An ascending city
Its tall houses rise
             white
Each by each
Overlaid with olive leaves

A city of Gypsies
Tired flowers in washed rags
Climbing steep alleys
To the caves of their sacred
         mountain
       ~

Once I walked in whispers
Through Granada's streets
Thought on curves:
A fan, a spine, a dancer's skirt
A muezzin's winding call

Then I walked to the Alhambra
A fortress that trapped my eyes
         in Islam
On the outside
     red and menacing
Within
A lacework palace
A sudden glance might shatter

Beneath its vaulted ceilings
White birds flew
Through arching windows
Trailing stories of crescent moons
Of blind musicians playing
           for the harems
Of Boabdil weeping
As his caliphate
     was conquered
       ~

At night
When it was silent
(the moon rests its case)
I beheld azure pools
Ran my fingers through troughs
        of water
Heard the music of the fountain
        spray

As shadows moved across the
        water
I watched a doorway
I dared not enter
(it was too seductive)
And left the palace
Full blown roses falling on my
        shoulders.

Vanishing

On hills spotted as a
      beetle's back
With olive trees

In white villages
Quiet like the step
Of ghosts

Black-winged women
Thin as needles
Walk
Saying little
Who lives...
Who dies...

But these villages
Absorbing light
Losing shadows
Are vanishing

Their bleached bones and
      walls
Are ceasing and becoming
      soil
     ~
Nothing left
Of days the sun
Stood on white
    legs
I resist the
      change
Lapse into alone

Into losses
Slim fissures
Tears
That have stayed
    a while.

II. GYPSIES

Fingers

Father Bartolo always had trouble with the unwritten rules of his church. Patagonia was his first pastoral assignment. But when he saw children starving under the Argentine dictatorship, he began smuggling munitions to the guerillas.

Newspapers reported on the activist priests. But the Vatican kept silent. That should have warned Father Bartolo; he was reassigned to a parish in Spain, one in the poorest and shabbiest barrio of Sevilla, with a declining attendance and a budget perennially in the red.

His parishioners were the beggars and derelicts who sang on street corners for a drink, the inhabitants and habitués of the brothels, and the Gypsies.

Now as Father Bartolo sat listening to Ana Maria, one of the Gypsy children in his parish, he folded his hands. It kept them from shaking. When Ana Maria told him about her grandmother talking to her from the grave, he didn't argue with her. When she told him about her grandmother's avenging *Mulo*, he didn't say it hadn't happened. When Ana Maria told him her Uncle Aurelio had cut off his own finger to keep his mother's, Magdalena's, *Mulo* from rising, he listened respectfully.

Father Bartolo had asked Ana Maria into his office, intending to cleanse her of her heretical beliefs. Instead, he was finding himself fascinated with the occult traditions of the Gypsies. And in a situation he never expected to be—tempted to mix the Word with Gypsy practices.

~

Ana Maria speaks: *Grandma's been calling my name the way she used to when she wanted to tell me something. So a week ago my Aunt Pastora took me to the cemetery. I sat down at the end of Grandma's grave and I said* Hello, Grandma. *I know she heard me 'cause the ground shook.*

Then I asked her what was it like to be dead. She said it was lonely, and she wanted to go to Glory. But she couldn't. She was trapped as long as Uncle Aurelio's finger was in front of her grave. She told me to take it away.

I didn't want to take away Uncle Aurelio's finger 'cause if Grandma goes to Glory, I can't talk to her anymore. But I knew I had to if she asked me. So I said I would if she promised she wouldn't send her Mulo *after Uncle Aurelio anymore. She promised. And I believed her 'cause he paid the price.*

Then I dug in the dirt in front of the tombstone for the finger. When I found it, it was all wrinkled and black and shorter than any of my fingers. I didn't want to touch it. But I picked it up with a leaf and took it home.

I didn't want to ever see it again. So I gave it back to Uncle Aurelio.

Uncle Aurelio is really unhappy 'cause he can't play the guitar anymore. It's been a month since my grandma died. She died 'cause Uncle Aurelio left our clan. That made a hole for the Evil One to get in, and then Grandma died. It's all his fault. That's why Grandma sent her Mulo *after him. Now Uncle Aurelio is back, though he doesn't do anything. He just sits all day in his little room with his guitar on his lap.*

~

Aurelio occupied himself with visions of his fingers flexing, spreading, fluttering; his index fingers, his ring fingers, his little fingers shifting rapidly across the strings of his guitar, his right thumb arching as he strummed a *rasqueada*.

Mostly he thought about the middle finger of his left hand.

When he cut it off he had not been aware of pain. Wrapping his hand tightly in a white handkerchief, watching the red stain smear, he thought it had to be someone else's blood, not his. Burying the finger in front of his mother's grave, this could not be happening to him. Later when he felt the pain and the long, low ache not only of the stump but of the absent finger he knew for a certainty that it was his own finger. He swore it was still there; he could still feel its fingertip itching and the nail growing.

But when Ana Maria gave the wrinkled stub back to him, he paid little attention to it. Putting it on a plate at the end of his window sill, he wasn't aware that its nail, still pink, had grown to a point. Nor that every night the stub, using the tip to spike the sill, was pulling the rest of itself along, humping and lowering like an inchworm.

The finger would walk the length of the window sill and back again until dawn. Then exhausted, it would pull itself up onto the plate, where it remained until the next night's walk.

The finger, mute, eyeless, earless, unable to verbalize, didn't know what it wanted. It could only yearn: there was something it must attach itself to, something it belonged with.

~

Ana Maria speaks: *Grandma called my name again. So I went back to the cemetery. Grandma said now she had a demon, and she couldn't go to Glory even with the finger gone. She said she was hearing all of the music Uncle Aurelio had ever played all at the same time, every note he ever practiced and every performance he ever gave. And it was getting louder and louder. She told me to go to Father Bartolo at the church and tell him to do something. So I did.*

~

Later that same day, Father Bartolo stood at the foot of Magdalena's grave and called out her name.

When he felt a slight tremor under his feet, he proceeded. "Magdalena, hear me: The demon in you cannot be exorcised until you have forgiven Aurelio."

This time the earth didn't tremble—it shook, it rumbled, it spit, it hissed, it boiled, and it roiled. Father Bartolo barely kept his footing. But he went on, "Magdalena, I am only telling you what the spirits say. You have to make up for what you did to Aurelio before you can go to Glory!

"You must draw on the rites and rituals of your tribe; you must beseech your dead ancestors; you must repeat the healing incantations of your clan. And you must do this until Aurelio is able to play the guitar again!"

~

Ana Maria speaks: *I guess Grandma did what Father Bartolo said she should, 'cause yesterday Uncle Aurelio came out of his room for the first time since he cut off his finger. He had a suitcase, and he said he was going to find a doctor who could sew the stub back on. Aunt Pastora thought that was a good idea. My uncle Pepino said the whole thing was stupid.*

On the bus, Aurelio kept the little stub in his left pants pocket. The stub could feel his left hand come in and out of the pocket, could feel the warmth of its flesh.

In Cádiz, Aurelio went down the list of surgeons in the telephone directory. Dr. Amador said it was impossible to sew the stub back on. Dr. Bernal said it would be unethical to even attempt it.

Dr. Claro asked Aurelio, "Haven't you ever heard of Django Reinhardt?"

Dr. Espin laughed at Aurelio.

But Dr. Fernandez said, "Come in. Let's talk."

Dr. Fernandez examined Aurelio's left hand and the dismembered finger very carefully. He sat, afterward, at his desk with his chin resting on his folded hands. Finally, he looked up at Aurelio and shook his head. "No," he said, "it's been way too long. It can't be done. But just for my own purposes, I would like to buy the stub of your finger to study."

Aurelio's back stiffened. "It's my finger and I'm not selling it!"

That night, Aurelio, afraid the doctor would steal it from him, slept with the stub under his pillow.

During the night Aurelio turned over on his face and stretched out his maimed hand alongside the pillow. The stub, sensing the warmth of the hand, crawled out from under the pillow next to the stump.

In the morning Aurelio wrapped his handkerchief around the stub and the stump so they would grow back together.

~

Ana Maria speaks: *Uncle Aurelio is home with his hand in a handkerchief. He walks around with that black finger sticking straight up in the air. He says it's growing back on his hand, and soon he'll be able to play the guitar again. Aunt Pastora thinks it's wonderful. But Uncle Pepino's really getting mad 'cause the finger keeps falling off Uncle Aurelio's hand. Once it fell in the* cocido *Aunt Pastora was cooking on the stove. Another time, Uncle Pepino found it on the bathroom floor. He almost had it flushed when Uncle Aurelio ran in and got it.*

~

After about a week it became apparent, even to Aurelio, that the finger and the stump were not growing back together. Aurelio placed the stump on the plate on his window sill again.

He had never asked himself how, in Cádiz, the finger had gotten out from under his pillow and next to the stump. But one night the question woke him up.

Aurelio, sitting up to think, his head propped on the pillow, noticed something moving on his window sill. Assuming it was a mouse, or worse, he got up and took a shoe to kill it. That's when he saw the stub of his finger plodding slowly back and forth across the sill.

Pulling up a chair, he sat and watched it until dawn. Gradually, he realized that every time the stub moved, the other fingers on his left hand would twitch.

~

Pepino, Aurelio's brother, knew the history of every clan in Spain and France. He knew how certain Gypsies had become famous and, by Gypsy standards, wealthy. Pepino knew all about Django Reinhardt.

When Aurelio asked him the question, Pepino replied, "Eh, what do you want to know about Django for?"

"He played the guitar without any fingers."

"Aurelio, don't be an idiot. Of course he had fingers. Two on his left hand. So why do you want to know?"

"Why? Why do you think? I've got three fingers on my left hand. That's one more than Django. And I want to play the guitar again. That's why!"

"Aurelio, you're too lazy. Django, he worked night and day, ten hours a day so he could play again. You haven't got the guts."

But Aurelio had an asset Pepino didn't know about.

From then on, every night, Aurelio sat in front of the window sill until dawn, holding his guitar and watching the stub walking back and forth.

After thirty-three years of playing the guitar, Aurelio had come to trust his fingers to know the strings better than he did. It came as no surprise to him that they communicated with one another, that they were able to compensate for each other if one was weak or tired.

Now, night after night, the important middle finger on the window sill was sending messages to its companions on his left hand.

At first, the three other fingers did little more than twitch. But slowly they found the strings again, responded to the stub, telling them how and where to move in its absence.

The more Aurelio's good fingers were able to play the guitar, the less the stub walked the window sill. Finally, it was staying all night on the plate, visibly growing smaller and smaller.

~

Ana Maria speaks: *The next time I went to the cemetery I went with flowers. But I had something else with me. Uncle Aurelio, when I told him Grandma had gone to Glory, gave me back the little stub of his finger. It was even littler now, no bigger than a button.*

When we got to the cemetery, I could tell Grandma was gone. So I buried Uncle Aurelio's finger in front of her gravestone. It belongs there.

The Gypsy Women

I loved the throbbing faces
Skull eyes leaning on big
    cheek bones
Mouths swelling with song

Leaning forward in small
    wooden chairs
Hands pressed hard on their
    heavy thighs
They passed around the pain

As the words came out
In knots and pieces
Echoing losses
The whole long night

But at dawn
The pain abating
They sat back
Hands folded, faces radiant
Patient with the world.

The Gypsy Men

They sat their big bellies on
   their thighs
And with faces
   rolls of fat or
   rutted cranky ridges
They sang

Cursing the hard rocks of
   their lives
As the night wore long
Lamenting in biting snippy
   protests
Lost loves and salted wounds

But with the dawn
Anger fading
They turned to clowning,
Danced a bawdy outcropping of
   bumps and grinds

And finished the night
With ribald wit
Sly eyes
And waggish faces.

Black and White:

The Women

A guitar is a black shadow on the white wall.

In the empty, sunlit streets, white house
      by white house, row on row
         of black doorways

Through the open street, unaltered,
A space of everything older,
Lived through twice,
Ghosts in black dresses cross
         doorway to doorway

Women, big women in round bodies,
White hair vanishing into white walls.
Women pass, touch hands, drop words

I walk the narrow curling streets,
I see no one.
But I can hear the women moving
Through the doorways, into the sinking houses.

Black and White:

The Storks

White knives in the sky,
Bones flying,
Arrow shafts with wedged heads,
Black wings and white bellies
They leave tracks behind them
         in the air

Dive like sea birds into
Trees, the solitary nesting trees,
Black spheres on slender crooked trunks
Paper cutouts by a child
On a golden landscape.

Black and White:

The Men in the Bar

Three. They talk with their hands,
Eat olives, and in-between, sing
Its fleshy bitter aromatic bite.

These men
In black suits with shiny seats and elbows
Are thin-limbed, with lantern jaws, yellow teeth.
They sing of dying love, and death.

But their song, like a fisherman's line,
Is a clear passage.
It can be followed to its end.
It secures the dark night
To the rims of their wine glasses.

Three Women:

1. Aurora

There was no record of her birth
She was a Gypsy

As a young girl
Face round
A fleshy apple
Aurora sang
Voice high, baby sweet
 an arrow to open the
        sky

As a woman
(A slim tree)
She married the little seed—
They held hands
Made gentle jokes
Her height, his nose

Every night she rocked beneath
        him
Every night she wished for
        a baby
None came

She knew the superstitions
        of her clan:
Garlic in belly buttons
Cures bed-wetting
Thorn bushes on gravestones
Keep the ghosts from rising

~

So she buried an egg
In the river's bank
Sat beside it day and
            night
Begging for a baby
None came

While in bed
She began to hear the
                extra beat
Of her husband's heart
That told her: other women

Undone
Her shadow let loose
Treading black
The weight began
Collapsed flesh
Jowls hanging from her jaw
Breasts sagging to her waist
Corpulence as a landscape:
            sea of belly
            terrain of hips
She could not sleep lying down
She'd suffocate

Still a kindly woman
Watching over everyone
She held together
The bits and pieces of her
            husband's life
Lying in the gutter like
                spangles off a
                    dress

~

The first attack
Her lights
All but gone
I held the sweaty head
    against
     my shoulder
While her heart turned
      over
       ~

The date of her dying is written
      in a book
The illness, the hospital, the doctor
       present
But her birth was never recorded
She was a Gypsy.

2. Evalina

Evalina's house is the sadness
        of parting
For goodbyes I claim
The vacant plaza
The back street
Where Evalina lived

The German jewess
Hiding from memories
Mistress of her circle
Small prophet surrounding
        herself
With Gypsies

At her double door
Cow bell clanking
She used to greet me
(Que venga, Doloré)

Lead me
Through her rooms
(Glowing yellow like
        cholla blossoms)
And out to her patio

Where old Gypsy saints
        sang
From the bottoms of their
        throats
While I rapped the rhythms on
        a tabletop

~

The rhythms still rattle
                  in my dreams
In a broken drawer
I keep a torn silk shawl

Cheap plastic earrings
A program from the *festival*
          at Ronda
The Gypsies' names signed
            with X's

Around my wrist
I wear the silver bracelet
Evalina gave me when
        I left

Its dark recesses
Its half circle remind me
I'm half a world away from Spain.

3. Lucy

She was the sadness
Of the scent of oranges
Of chiffon skirts
               clinging
As she walked along the
        river

Her moods were illusive
A smile foreign to her
Yet she smiled often

Through the long nights of
         song
One man was always by
         her side
A Gypsy
His face a golden color
His arms were shaped to
           hold the guitar

But come nights of
Pale green and pink lights
He left her for another
   on Christmas eve

       ~

Lucy
Thin
Delicate
Reclining on a couch
Under mellow lamps
(Crushed velvet, pomegranates)
She was the dark thread
      struck
The dark thread I loved.

News From Sevilla

1.

Juanito and Lucy
Never one without
    the other

He
The balding Gypsy
Pursed lips
Light heart
His songs
Sparks
      between the
          beats

She
The dancer
Her heels a
      crackle of
         lace
On a wooden floor

After twenty years
Of living together
           in sin
A delicious wobbly joyous
        sin
They marry.

2.

Evalina
Has died

Having lived and thought
       gratefully
She refused chemo

I recall
Her cock's comb of red hair
The freckled face
Frisky knees and
            elbows

Her quick house
The loud cowbell
At her door

The patio
With its in and out
Of Gypsies

I remember
The music they brought
The poetry they left.

3.

Mario
He knew the life
            of music
The painful details
All of them

The word around
            says
His mind is gone

But I recall
His taut angles
Clean black line of
            clothing
Lean hands
Balanced on the strings
            of his guitar

I remember
The monastery garden
That night he played
            the Rodrigo
And the old stones
            melted.

            ~

It is said
We cannot go back

Yet I do
To light nights
And wealth of friends.

Carmen Amaya

*Carmen Amaya, 1913-1963, a Barcelona Gypsy,
brought to flamenco her fierce spirit, and a long line
of flamenco artists.*

Rattling her heels
As if they would
    shatter
Her small tight
        bee body
She danced up and
    down
The black hill of
        Montjuich

Her clan
Out of reach of
    rules
But not fire bombs
And threats
(the old father disappeared
was never seen again)
Finally left Barcelona

With Carmen
In the lead
They traveled slowly
    south
Their wagons
Pulled by mules
Better fed than they were

~

In Andalucia
They lived in caves
Filled with fleas and rats
Lit fires
Sat and sang
Their heavy gold
Held each other in their
            misery

In time the clan
Breaking open the courteous
            flamenco
That had no desperate need
                to be
Produced
Singers, guitarists, dancers
All in Carmen's name
            ~
Today the clan is affluent
As Gypsies go
Today they trim lavender
And talk to Carmen
In her grave.

Diego del Gastor

Diego del Gastor, a Gypsy, died in 1975. For fifty years he was the dominant flamenco guitarist of Spain, rarely leaving his hometown.

Crowds followed him like
    a halo
With his sunken cheeks
    owl eyes
And white suits
He was never hard to find

Guitar joined at the
    breastbone
He played in the bars and plazas
From three every afternoon
Till three the next morning
Took no money for his music
It was his art
    he said

Spider hands
Crawling the frets
His music twanged
    the ears
Bent the rhythms
Where others only walked
His sound skipped and
    trembled

~

Half smiling from his
                  monk place
He played if no one
                  was listening
When everyone was
        listening

Sitting sideways in
                  their chairs
Aficionados leaned
                  to hear him
He would never die
                they said

But the night the moon
Came up black
He did die
Seated upright in
        his chair
Head bent over his
        guitar.

Pepe Rios

Pepe Rios Amaya, Gypsy, date of birth unknown, died in 1995. A rhythmic genius, he was noted for his heelwork.

In his youth
Small and slim
He could flash on any
     stage
Scuttle with the swiftness
     of an insect

Chattering his heels
He gathered rhythms
From the click of fingernails
Jingle of jewelry
Buzz of a spotlight

Where others heard
       only chaos
He always found
    the beat.

As an old man
Grown even smaller
Skinny arms hanging
    hairy
Beer belly bulging
He danced at night
    in bars
Found Sevilla's
    beat:

Staccato street talk
Flutter of silk fans
Clatter of hooves on
                    cobblestones
Spurt of blood in the
        bullring

Dancing
In spaces barely
                    wider
Than he was
His heels still
Sounded to the center
        of the earth

Still timed
The movement of the
            stars.

III. MOODS

Evil Eye

The Gypsies say it is unlucky to meet a monk or priest first thing in the morning; nothing will go right the rest of the day.

~

Old Maudi sat all day every day on Sierpes, the serpentine walking street of Sevilla. She sold bruised apples, stale bread, used shoes, and anything else she could find after the flea markets closed.

Maudi had a shriveled face, an unkempt, tangled mass of gray hair, and the Evil Eye. But she kept that for special occasions. Usually she would only hiss at people who passed her and didn't buy.

Sitting all day on the sidewalk without food or water, she had only a bowl of salt by her side in which she would now and then dip her fingers, then lick them clean. At night she went home to a room in a condemned building. She had no light, no heat, no water; her bed was a straw mattress on the floor. For cooking, there was an iron fire box on the shelf where she kept one spoon, one fork, one knife, a cracked plate, a dirty frying pan, and a stew pot large enough to stew two whole chickens.

But she never used the stew pot because it was stuffed with money. Her joy was to take the bills out of the pot, smooth them with her hands, and look at each one. She talked to the bills, clucking over a smudge, mark, or tear, told each one its story: where it had been, what it had seen, and how sadly it had been treated—crushed, crumpled, and dirtied—until it finally found safety in her pot.

Maudi loved her money and would never spend it. Least of all did she give any to Father Bartolo who certainly knew of old Maudi. But Maudi would have nothing to do with him. Once when Father Bartolo

69

invited her to a church supper, she threw salt in his face.

But Father Bartolo was not easily put off. Every time he was on Sierpes, he would stop, buy something from her, and tell her the parish would gladly offer her food and clothing, with no strings attached. Maudi would have none of it.

Father Bartolo spent his mornings on Sierpes cajoling money from the owners of the posh stores, and from the affluent Spaniards, those men in the private clubs who stared all day at the street through one-way windows.

Once in a while he had a profitable morning. It was on one of those days when Father Bartolo was feeling particularly good, even jovial, that he decided on a new approach to Maudi. He had bargained; he had argued; he had pleaded. But he had never teased her: "Eh, Maudi, I'm collecting for the church. Why don't you give me your money," he said, and held out his hand.

Old Maudi looking up at him with those odd green eyes of hers was the last thing Father Bartolo remembered before finding himself inexplicably back in his Parish office, and invisible.

Absentmindedly, he had reached out his hand to turn the pages of his appointment book, and gasped. He could feel his hand, its weight and substance, flesh and bone—but he couldn't see it. He looked at his wrist, forearm, and elbow. Nothing.

In the small mirror on the wall, he saw no image. Yet when he touched his face, he could feel his features, the beginnings of stubble on his chin, the sweat running down his cheeks. Oh my God, oh my God, he tried saying aloud—he couldn't hear his own voice either—as he sat down heavily in a chair.

~

Ana Maria speaks: *Since Grandma died, I've been lonely. I used to talk to her all the time when I lived in Calatrava, and she taught me to read the signs and omens. But staying with my Uncle Pepino and my Aunt Pastora, there's lots to do in Sevilla. I go to Sierpes almost every day to look at the store windows and buy a cookie at the bakery. Whenever I pass old Maudi, she hisses at me. But I just hiss back at her.*

One day when I hissed at her, she threw the Evil Eye on me. But I threw it right back; my grandma taught me how. Then Maudi said to me, Cale? *And I answered her,* Sí, I'm Gypsy, too. *And since then she hasn't used the Evil Eye on me.*

The Evil Eye is dangerous. It made me sick when I was little. Someone threw it on me 'cause they were mad at my clan. But my grandma ran ice water on the edge of a knife and I got well. Now I wear my amulet all the time.

My Uncle Anzo wasn't wearing an amulet when someone threw the Evil Eye on him. He went walking in the woods one day and never came back.

Now no one has seen Father Bartolo for days and I'm thinking old Maudi threw the Evil Eye on him.

Anyway, last week when I went to Sierpes, I said hello to Maudi and she said hello back and gave me an apple. So I went in the bakery and bought two cookies and gave her one. Then I started going to Sierpes just to see Maudi.

But my Aunt Pastora shakes her head and says I should stay away from her.

~

The first time Maudi went to the Prado Museum, she stood for hours in front of the Hieronymus Bosch and Goya paintings. Staring at Bosch's broken egg shells and skulls, she flew the dark sky with his monsters. She stirred the cauldron with Goya's witches.

Maudi believed only in the power of Evil. With her Evil Eye she could make children fall ill with strange fevers, horses and mules go blind, pregnant women miscarry. She could turn water poisonous, sink boats, and collapse caves. And she could make certain people, as she put it, *go away.*

Still better, she could sit on her straw bed and fly her pot of money across the room into her arms.

But as much as she loved the money, it was not her greatest treasure. That she kept in an old coffee pot.

Once a week Maudi would catch a mouse in the basement of her building and carry it wiggling in her hand to the coffee pot on her shelf. Opening the lid, she would feed the mouse to the small black snake coiled in the pot, and watch as it unlocked its jaw and swallowed the mouse whole.

Then Maudi would take out the snake, kiss it on its dry cold mouth, and coo to it as it made its way up her arm to her neck.

Maudi tingled all over as she felt its ribs walking up her arm and on her neck, felt its forked tongue shooting deep into her ear. And then there was the pleasant warmth as it coiled itself up in her bush of hair.

Before going to bed, she would gently pull it out of her hair and wash its whole head with her tongue. Maudi knew that it was her weekly love-making with her black snake that recharged her power, a luminous force at the base of her spine that she could turn dark as night.

Maudi was the mistress of her black craft. But she had never had an apprentice. Or even thought of one, until the little girl came by who could throw Maudi's Evil Eye right back at her.

~

Ana Maria speaks: *I didn't see old Maudi for a few days. But then Aunt Pastora wanted me to go to the bakery and there Maudi was.*

I said hello and she said I should come see her room where she lived. But I told Maudi that my Aunt Pastora said I shouldn't go.

Then Maudi said if I wanted her to, she could make Aunt Pastora go away.

I'm sure old Maudi made Father Bartolo invisible. And if Maudi, she got mad enough at Aunt Pastora, she'd make her invisible too. So I thought I'd better go see Maudi's room like she wanted.

When I got there, the room was dark and smelly. I wanted to go home. But then she showed me her snake. In Calatrava, there are always snakes in the garden. I play with them. So when I saw the snake in Maudi's coffee pot, I took it out and let it wrap itself around my hands. I think the snake liked me better than Maudi 'cause when Maudi tried to take it back, it hissed at her.

Maudi got very angry and I thought she was going to throw the Evil Eye on me. But she couldn't, 'cause as long as I had her snake, Maudi didn't have the Evil Eye.

So I held onto the snake. Then Maudi took a bowl of salt off her shelf and said she'd give it to me if I gave back her snake. But I said my Aunt Pastora has a whole box of salt in her kitchen, so I didn't need Maudi's.

Then Maudi took the big pot off her shelf and said she'd give me what was inside. When she opened the pot, it was full of money. I've never seen so much money. I thought about taking it; I know how much my Uncle Pepino likes money. But my mama always says money causes more problems than it cures.

So I told Maudi that when she made Father Bartolo visible again, I'd give her back her snake. Then I ran out of the room and all the way home. And I put the snake in my closet. But it crawled out and went in

Uncle Pepino's bedroom.

The next day, Aunt Pastora and I went to the park. I decided to take the snake with me 'cause I didn't trust Uncle Pepino. He was very upset when he found it in his bed.

Anyway, I put the snake in the pocket of my dress. The pocket that has a little hole in it.

When we got to the park, Aunt Pastora sat on a bench but I sat on the ground. And guess what? The snake got out of that little tiny hole. I never saw it again. And I never saw old Maudi again either.

But Maudi must have thought she was going to get her snake back 'cause the next day Father Bartolo was in the barrio and telling everybody he had just gone on a short vacation. But I know better.

No one sees old Maudi anymore on Sierpes. Her building has been torn down and Maudi is gone, and so is her pot of money.

Epilogue

Every morning in Madrid, a taxi pulls up to the main entrance of the Prado. The museum guards smile as they open the door for the little old lady who lives at the Ritz Hotel.

Dressed in a silk couture suit, a cashmere stole around her shoulders, a small mink hat set on her meticulously coifed hair, she makes her way down the wide corridors tapping her walking stick, the one with the solid gold snake's head, until she reaches the Bosch and Goya paintings.

There she stands for hours, staring at the paintings and talking to the snake's head. Now and then she reaches into the bottom of her Gucci purse, takes out a tiny bowl of salt, dips in her fingers, and licks them clean.

Los Naranjos

They amaze me:
These trees
Come Christmas
Or nearly
The bitter green pebbles
Break into bright
                 orange
Mix their color
With the grey dusty smoke
From roasting chestnuts

And behind that
Or through that
Brittle Christmas
                 lights
Prickle the eyes

A photo brings it back
How something so
                 common
Just tree after tree
Laden with oranges
Can make Spain happen.

Guadalquivir

Luminous river of Spain
Steel blue in the morning
        cool
There I begin my walk
Search its depths
        for answers

History clings to the river
Cortes, Magellan, Pizarro
Set sail on it
Columbus returned on its tides

But dark trees rode the landscape
Old Spain reveling in stolen
        gold
Lost its century
To the weight of conquest

I walk on
And seek the river under Islam

At dusk its color dims
At dusk if no tumult broke its
        peace
Ancient Arabs sat cross-legged
        on the quay
Worshiped water
Listened to the lute
And watched barefoot dancers

Yet the Christian monarchs
Cast out the crescent moon
That gave the curve
        to Spain

I walk on
It is night
The river is deep blue
I will cross a bridge
Look down at these waters

75

Horse-drawn carriages pass me by
Animal odors mix with cooler air
On the quay four women dance
            April-eyed
Faces illumined by paper
            lanterns

Along the bank
The Gypsies
Mud-spattered
Sit and sing flamenco

Yowling the belly songs
            of sorrow
Their voices shiver with
                  the river's mist
Sing of lives upside down
In the days and nights
            of Franco
Of the rubble of caves and
            dead horses

I walk on
It is midnight
The waters have darkened to indigo
And although the river is quiet
Without menace
It is deep with disasters
            ~
Barefoot on its bank
The pebbles of recollection may cut
                  my feet
But I will follow the river's blue
Wherever
It takes me.

Moods:

1. Convent in Vejer

Crowned in pearls
A woman sits like a stone in the
               wind
And waits for the world

Jagged lines of light illumine her
           black marble hair
Her shoulders slope to ivory hands
           holding the Child

Behind her
Waiting on the white wall
A long-legged spider
Kneels to her shadow.

2. Dancer On The Beach

The fishing boats slip back and forth
Leave black reflections in the pale blue
     water
While fishermen walk in the waist-high sea
  white shirts catching the wind
        like sails

On the shore
The dancer's feet carve circles
   in the sand
While her fingers rap the air
Search the sky for rhythms
That call the fish from the sea.

3. Spanish Tapestry

The old guitarist sits beside the
        barefoot dancer
As air ripples the flesh and beach water
        laps at the heels
His trills insinuate an amorous intent:
Palm trees, red petals, on black silk

Scent of sweet oil, skin of dark honey
        lips of wet roses
Arms writhing
Hips shifting
The dancer moves from leg to leg in
        an easy rhythm
While sloe-eyed Arab friends
Sitting cross-legged on a carpet
Sip red wine from her slippers.

Festival at Ronda

Ledge city
Time has ridden it away
Twenty-five hundred feet above
          the valley floor
Ancient, mythic, lone
Its dimensions fade
Edges blur, houses merge

In the mornings
The streets grow whiter
As they're walked through
Give small prizes
(Green stable doors for burros
Red geraniums for landmarks)
As I pass spindle-legged women
          all in black
Who chatter, laugh, dodge
          my shadow

Late afternoons
I listen to the Spaniards talking
          in the bars
Watch their chiffon wives
(Bracelets jangling on their wrists)
Dance in high-heeled shoes

But I came to Ronda to hear
          the Gypsies sing
In the ice cool night
In Ronda's bullring
Its bleak flow of recent blood
          forgotten:

On a plain stage with klieg lights
The Gypsies gathering
Sometimes shrieking
They spill their feelings
In a wash of tremolos
In cracked and broken words:

La Perrata
Laying open her years
Brings old ghosts to heel
    "...and the wind said...what is the use of sighing..."

El Lebrijano
An elegant voice
All lace and stinging needles
    "...love destroys the senses...I talk from experience..."

Fernanda
Exploring the caves
Rolls darkness on her tongue
    "...you deceive me...and lies become truth..."

Bernarda
Piercing shrill
Finishes with joy
    "...there's a door to my soul that needs no key..."

~

I did not grow weary as the night
       grew long
And morning climbed the sky

In the crystal dawn
I stood with strangers on
             Ronda's cliff
Looked out across the great
                 abyss

And watched the Gypsies' children
Steer their goats across the
    valley floor.

The Widow

My village, it's common as salt

Even when there is talk
And there is always talk
Its streets are silent

I walk
Trailing shreds of black cloth
I carry lilies pressed against my
                    breasts
By night
They are empty moons

But by day
I shed my shadow on the streets
And gates open for me

I enter but do not stay
Others
They would have me talk
They quote, they guess
But I who know
Think,
He and I...we are together...we expect no changes

In the quiet of the
                    cemetery
There I can speak
Dig my fingers in
                    the black soil
Ask,
Are you there...still there?

Complaint

Clinging to the
      hills
Like low clouds
White ancient
       villages

                Deserted

Spotted as a beetle's back
With olive trees
The land

                Rotting

The sun's earthly
      children
Fields
Of turning yellow
      faces

                Charred black

The Gypsies' carved
      cliffs
And white-washed
      caves

                Abandoned

On rocky promontories
The curved walls
Of Arab castles

                In ruins

Spain's
Fragile beauties

                Ending.

Miracle Child

The Gypsies attribute mystical powers to all reflective surfaces: any reflection can absorb the soul of the one reflected.

~

Pastora had been married fifteen years and was childless. To her face, she was pitied by her clan. Behind her back, she was their shame.

Sitting on the riverbank next to the egg she had buried, Pastora left off counting the nights she and Pepino had slept together and not conceived. Instead, she began to count the stars.

But her mind, floating with the overlapping currents of the river, wandered toward sleep. *I mustn't sleep. I mustn't*, she told herself. The *bruja* had said, "Sit by the egg under the full moon, and the egg will enter you by first light."

At dawn, Pastora began to feel her belly weighing heavy as a rock; she felt luminous with child. "And this will be the proof you have conceived," the *bruja* had told her. "You will feel the child in your womb, and it will tell you its name."

Later that morning over breakfast, Pastora told Pepino she was pregnant.

"You can't be," he replied.

"I am."

"By who? We haven't slept together in years."

"By an egg, Pepino."

"You're talking nonsense."

"It's true, Pepino. It's a miracle child! The *bruja* told me."

"This is rot. If you're going to go to a *bruja,* at least don't believe what she tells you."

"You've gone to *brujas,* Pepino. Remember that time you couldn't get it up and you went to a *bruja* and she gave you some herbs and—"

"That was different. Besides, what do we need a baby for? We've gotten along fine without one. We've—"

But Pastora wasn't listening. She had started for the kitchen.

Pepino yelled at her, "Don't you leave me while I'm talking to you!"

"Why not? You do it to me."

"What's got into you?"

"I'm pregnant now, Pepino. I'm as good as any other woman in the clan, and I can walk away from you if I want to."

"No, you can't. Besides, you're not pregnant."

"Yes, I am."

And even with the passing months, even as her belly grew no bigger, Pastora was still convinced.

~

Ana Maria speaks: *My Aunt Pastora takes care of me and everybody else. But it doesn't make her any happier. Uncle Pepino always has other women.*

My mama says he's a libertino *and has a penis ten feet long. I don't see how that could be. I heard some people have tails, and they hang them down their trousers. But if Uncle Pepino put his penis down his trouser leg, it would still hang out over his shoes, and he'd be stepping on it all the time.*

Anyway, Uncle Pepino got mad 'cause Aunt Pastora said she was pregnant. He left and didn't come back for two days. Aunt Pastora had to borrow money from the neighbors to buy food.

~

At the end of the ninth month, Pastora went into labor. Although no baby was born, she felt it moving through the birth canal. She could hear it sucking air at the moment of birth, then crying.

Sitting up in bed, she wrapped her dream in a blanket, and named him Miguel Antonio.

At the same moment, the *puta,* Rosa, in a brothel six blocks away, was giving birth to a son whom she named Antonio Miguel. Rosa knew, although she didn't know how she knew, that it was not her baby being born but another woman's.

~

It was right after Antonio Miguel was born that Pastora began dreaming herself into Rosa's room. She dreamt it in detail, ran her fingers down the faded pink drapes, stroked the tattered fur throw on the bed, straightened the magenta silk coverlet. She stood looking down for a long moment at the tiny infant asleep in the pulled-out bottom drawer of the bureau, and when she looked up she watched as Pepino walked out of Rosa's room.

Soon afterward, Rosa dreamt herself into Pastora's flat. Crossing the living room, she entered the small bedroom where Pastora collected her tears, the room she no longer shared with Pepino. On a table waited a stack of neatly folded diapers and a row of clean baby bottles. Next to the table stood an empty crib.

Pastora and Rosa started talking. Pastora told Rosa about the baby's birth, how long she was in labor, how many pounds he weighed, all the time gazing down at the empty crib, while Rosa whispered baby noises at the small pillow and flat blanket.

Before long, Rosa and Pastora were meeting regularly in each other's dreams. They talked about Pepino: his moods, his needs, his obstinacy. They shared the intimacies of motherhood: the formulas, the rashes, the midnight feedings.

But one night, Rosa came crying to Pastora; there was trouble happening at the brothel.

The other *putas* had been keeping the madam away from Rosa's room, telling the madam wild stories about the cries she was hearing—a drunken client, a trapped cat in the alleyway. But one morning the madam looked in Rosa's room for herself. She told Rosa she had a week to give up the baby.

Pastora offered at once to take Antonio Miguel and Rosa agreed. It could all be so simple.

Except for Pepino.

~

In the morning over breakfast, Pastora said she was taking Rosa's baby.

"Rosa who? And no, you're not."

87

"You know, Rosa the *puta*."

Pepino choked on his coffee. "How do you know her?"

"We meet every night."

"You what?"

"We meet each other in our dreams. That's how I know she has my baby."

"What baby?"

"Yours, Pepino. You're the father."

"I am not!"

"Oh, I've seen you at the brothel, Pepino."

"What do you mean! And what are you doing in a brothel!"

"Oh, I saw you leaving Rosa's room. And Rosa wants me to take the baby and—"

"No. No. No! I don't believe any of this!"

~

That night before falling asleep, Pepino said to himself, *I don't dream. I won't dream.* But as soon as he closed his eyes, the dream descended on him. He dreamt he was in Rosa's room. Not that he minded, of course, but Pastora was there too. As soon as he saw her, Pepino wanted out. But he didn't know how to un-dream.

He watched speechless while Pastora and Rosa stood and talked to each other. Finally finding his voice, he squeaked, "What are you two talking about?"

"About the baby, what else?" Pastora replied.

"What baby?"

Rosa pointed to Antonio Miguel in the bottom drawer of her bureau. "That's your baby," Rosa said, "yours and Pastora's."

"Can't be."

"Is."

"Can't be. And anyway, I'm leaving this dream."

Pepino clapped his hands. He shouted. He stomped on the floor. Nothing woke him up. Then he tried climbing out of the dream by way of the window. He had one leg over the sill when he realized he was four flights up, and maybe dreams were more real than he thought.

Pepino climbed back into the room, sat down on the foot of the bed, looked up at Pastora and said, "All right, all right. You can have the baby."

But what Pepino did in the dream, he did not do in daylight. "No," he said to Pastora in the morning, "No! You can't have the baby and that's final!"

For the first time, Pastora's conviction faltered. Weeping, she went to Rosa's room in the brothel. "He won't! He won't!" she cried.

"We have to break his will," replied Rosa.

"How?"

"You tell me. You're the Gypsy."

So Pastora called the *bruja,* and the *bruja* told her it could all be done with mirrors.

~

Ana Maria speaks: *Nobody ever tells me anything. But I know Aunt Pastora and Rosa and the* bruja *are planning something. They want to change Uncle Pepino's mind about the baby. It has to do with mirrors.*

My mama says mirrors are dangerous. If you stand between two mirrors and see yourself a whole lot of times, the Evil One can get into you. And if you're looking in a mirror when it cracks all the way across, then you can get caught in the crack and you don't know who you are anymore. I think that's what's going to happen to Uncle Pepino.

~

That same night, Pastora waited outside Pepino's room, listening to his breathing.

As soon as she heard Pepino snoring, she hurried out of the flat. Taking a large jar with her, she headed down to the riverbank.

But Pepino, only pretending to sleep, had been listening for Pastora's footsteps. As soon as he heard Pastora leave, he got out of bed and went to Rosa's room.

Rosa welcomed him cordially. She plumped the pillows on her bed, brought him a glass of wine. She sat next to him, told him to lean back and get comfortable.

Encouraging Pepino to talk, she listened, clucking in sympathy when he complained about Pastora and her delusions. When his words began to slur, Rosa took away his glass of wine and slid down onto the bed.

Pepino, doing the same, looked up and saw himself in the big mirror on the ceiling.

~

Meanwhile, at the riverbank Pastora had dug a shallow round hole—it had to be perfectly round—and filled it with water. With only the moon for light, she crouched down and stared fixedly into the pool of water. She waited, barely breathing. She would have to be ready, and she would have to be quick.

And she was. As soon as Pepino saw himself in the mirror, his face appeared in the pool. Pastora, splashing the water as hard as she could with the heel of her hand, shattered the image.

At the same instant, the mirror in Rosa's room gave a loud crack and split from side to side.

Pepino, startled, rolled off the bed and onto the floor.

Pastora, trembling with excitement, filled the jar with the water. Screwing the lid on, she knew she had Pepino's soul, and his will.

~

In the morning at home, Pepino had no memory of what had happened the night before. He was happy with both himself and Pastora. He didn't curse when he cut himself shaving. He didn't blame Pastora when his shoelaces broke. He didn't scream at her when he found his money had slipped through the hole in his pocket she forgot to mend.

But he did have a vague feeling, like an itch he couldn't reach, that he had lost something. He didn't know what it was, nor did he have the least idea where to look for it.

Over breakfast, he listened quietly while Pastora talked on and on. To everything she said he replied, *yes, yes.* When she asked him if she could take the baby, *yes, yes.* When she asked if Rosa could bring it over that day, *yes, yes.*

~

Ana Maria speaks: *I have a new baby cousin! His name is Miguel Antonio Antonio Miguel. It's a little confusing 'cause Rosa gave birth to the baby but it's Aunt Pastora's by the egg she buried in the riverbank. But Uncle Pepino is really the father.*

Anyway, at the baptism, the church was full. All our clan was there.

90

Grandpa Joselero and Grandma Juana came and sang nanas *to the baby. And there was my Uncle Diego, who wouldn't go anywhere without his guitar. He sat tuning it the entire service.*

Aunt Pastora asked the bruja *to come too but she didn't tell the priest. The* bruja *sat right in the front row with Rosa and the other* putas. *When Uncle Pepino stood up with Aunt Pastora for the baptism, the* putas *all waved and blew him kisses.*

Afterward, we went into a big room in the church and everybody danced in a circle around Aunt Pastora and the baby. Aunt Pastora was crying 'cause she was so happy, and Uncle Pepino wanted everybody to know it was his baby. We all had a good time and Father Bartolo would have had a good time too except he drank too much and fell asleep.

Epilogue

The night of the baptism, Pastora sat up late in bed looking first at baby Miguel Antonio, then at the water-filled jar on her night table.

Pastora thought a long time about the way Pepino used to treat her, yelling at her, having his other women. But now with his will gone, it was true, he was different.

Life in the flat was very quiet. Pepino agreed with her on everything.

But what did it matter, Pastora wondered. It was like living with a cloud. There was nothing she could get hold of, nothing she could either love or hate.

Pastora sighed and reached over to the night table, unscrewed the lid of the jar, and emptied the water into the diaper pail. Then she turned off the light.

~

In the morning, Pepino howled when he cut himself shaving. He swore at Pastora when his shoelaces broke. He screamed at her for not mending the hole in his pocket.

But he never, from that day on, complained about the baby.

IV. DANCES

.

Tarot

The Tarot deck, its major arcana representing the twenty-two archetypes from the mystic Qabalah, has accompanied the Gypsies since their first migration to Spain in the fifteenth century.

~

Ana Maria speaks*: Father Bartolo's coming tonight. He wants Aunt Pastora to read his cards 'cause he thinks he wants to be a Gypsy.*

I like staying with my Uncle Pepino and Aunt Pastora, but sometimes at night when I can't sleep 'cause I miss my mama, I go out on the balcony and pretend I'm back in her kitchen. I can see the toad in the corner with a red string tied 'round its neck to protect us from the Evil One. And my mama, she's cooking a rabbit and she can tell from its guts who's going to die next. And if I twist a coin in my apron pocket, I can hear my uncle Joselero singing to me from Glory.

He sings about how we are the royal people 'cause God gave us powers that only the Gypsies have and Father Bartolo will never have. No one can be a Gypsy just 'cause they want to.

~

Pastora had not been able to do the one thing necessary to claim her right to be a member of her clan: she had not had children. The weight of this would have crushed her, except for her one talent. Every night, in a back room of her old flat in the oldest barrio of Sevilla, Pastora would read her clan's fortunes.

Sitting on boxes, the Gypsies would watch as Pastora laid out the Tarot cards in a wide arc on the floor.

The Gypsies, accustomed to interpreting pebbles, bird bones, goat

95

turds, the dried mud of puddles, accustomed to listening to the voices of the Dead and the Unborn, would sit patiently while Pastora, contemplating the cards, dreamt herself into them.

As they watched, her face would grow ashen as her features, dimming and shriveling, were being sucked into her skull. Gray dust would pervade the room as Pastora began to talk to each of the figures.

Slowly, from whatever card Pastora was looking at, a figure, opaque, fleshy, tall, towering over the Gypsies, would rise up.

Perhaps it would be the raggle-taggle Fool in his wildly colored patches. Or Strength in her voluminous red robes, her vision calm and serene. Perhaps it would be Justice, with her sour-dour face, a sword in one hand and scales in the other. Or the Devil, half naked, blue-bodied, bat-winged, a second pair of eyes leering out of his kneecaps.

Unafraid, neither disturbed nor disbelieving, the Gypsies would wait for Pastora to explain the meaning of what they were seeing.

She always spoke to them in symbols: "The Fool is telling you, Manolo, there are dead flowers on the path you're taking." "Elena, Strength says kill the scorpions in your house before they kill you!" "Mercedes, don't listen to the Devil. Seek the shadows, not sunlight, or you will lose your own soul."

When the reading was over, Pastora, her face gradually resuming its natural contours, would raise a finger and summon each figure to wither and descend back down into its card on the floor.

Then, quietly spreading the cards again in a neat arc, she would leave the room as if nothing had happened.

~

Father Bartolo never expected to be attracted to the Gypsies. It was his intention to cleanse his Gypsy parishioners of their heretical beliefs. Instead, he found himself attracted to their mysterious powers. Soon, rumors were reaching the Bishop that he was mixing the Word with occult practices.

Father Bartolo, called into the Bishop's office, spoke honestly, telling the Bishop everything he had been involved in since the first Gypsy family came to his parish: an avenging ghost he had placated by granting it absolution; a miracle baby, conceived by an egg having been buried in the river bank, whom he baptized; a postmortem exorcism that he conducted to rid a recently deceased Gypsy of a demon.

Within ten days of talking to the Bishop, Father Bartolo was relieved of his parish duties as well as his income and was living in one small, drab room in the barrio.

He thought of suicide and dismissed the idea; it wasn't allowed in his religion. Neither was dabbling in Gypsy practices. But he had already crossed that line.

~

It was late at night when Father Bartolo came to Pastora. He walked the long hallway to the back room, dragging his fingers along the wall, wondering if the cards could tell him if he was really ready to leave his religion for that of the Gypsies'—occult, grotesque, unrepentant, and unshriven.

In Pastora's room, he tried to wait calmly, not understanding why Pastora was sniffling and tearing at her Kleenex. When she finally got the words out—Pepino had told her that anyone who was not Gypsy had to pay for the reading—Father Bartolo patted her on the hand and assured her that he was perfectly willing to pay.

Then in silence, Pastora laid out the cards, focusing on one card in particular. As she stared at it, the Hermit, an old man tried and tired, not belonging to anyone but himself, gathering his robes about him and holding a lantern, rose up out of the card.

Not knowing which frightened him more, the figure looming over him or Pastora's face shrinking into her skull, Father Bartolo bolted from the room, ran down the long hallway, down two flights of stairs, and out of the building.

Father Bartolo saw old Sevilla as his landscape of Hell. Expecting the Hermit to suddenly appear from behind trees or out of doorways, he ran—he didn't know where—until he finally came to a familiar doorway and burst through it.

Entering the sanctuary of what had once been his own parish church, he collapsed into the nearest pew.

Putting his face in his sweaty hands, he tried not to see the figure that was slowly rising in the aisle next to him.

It was a long time before Father Bartolo dared to look up at the old Hermit. When he did, although still frightened, he saw there was neither danger nor menace in its heavily lined eyes.

But there was certainly a message: he must admit to himself, then and there, that he was no Gypsy. And he must find his way, the Hermit's way, back to his own religion.

Several hours and a lot of prayer later, Father Bartolo looked up again and noticed, dispassionately, that the figure of the Hermit had diminished until it was no more than a spot on the carpet.

The next morning, Father Bartolo wrote two letters, one to the Bishop asking his blessing for what he was about to do. And the other to a medieval city in the far northwest corner of Spain.

~

Ana Maria speaks: *Aunt Pastora and Uncle Pepino got into a big fight over Father Bartolo. Uncle Pepino had said anybody who isn't Gypsy had to pay for the reading or Uncle Pepino would lock the room and Aunt Pastora could never read the cards again. Well, Father Bartolo left Aunt Pastora's reading in a hurry and didn't pay her. So Uncle Pepino is really mad. He put big boards across the door to the back room and nailed it shut. Aunt Pastora, she just sat down outside the room and cried and cried.*

~

Pastora's tears running in torrents through the keyhole, soaking the cards on the floor, animated the figures. Rising up from the cards with macabre energy, Chariot overran World, the Emperor strangled Temperance, the High Pope wrestled Justice to the floor, and the Lovers fought as Death was mangling the Magician with his scythe.

Pastora, terrified, could feel the waves of their fury coming through the door, threatening to inflame the entire flat.

Pepino, seeing the walls of the flat turning red, ran down the hall and with his bare hands pulled the heavy boards off the door.

Pastora stood up in the open doorway and boldly stared down the figures until they retreated, deflated and docile, each to its own card on the floor. Then, the heat subsiding, Pastora left the room, its door unlocked.

~

Several weeks after Father Bartolo had seen the Hermit, he arrived in the northwest corner of Spain in the province of Galicia. At the door to the Monastery of Antealtares, across the plaza from the great Cathedral of Santiago de Compostela, he handed over his worldly possessions—a few books, a few clothes—to the Brother Prior. Then he gave him an envelope addressed to Pastora and asked the Prior to mail it.

~

Ana Maria speaks: *Father Bartolo is gone and he's not coming back. That's what he said in a letter to Aunt Pastora. She can't read or write so I had to read the letter to her. He thanked her for what she tried to do but he said he was no Gypsy. Well, I knew that all along. Anyway, Aunt Pastora's really happy 'cause he also sent her some money and 'cause Uncle Pepino, he's never said another word to her about the readings.*

Gypsy Flamenco

Torn corner of a
      moment
Raving women dance
Wheel their arms
In perpetual prayer

Stockings shredded
Skirts torn
Shoes like
      cloven hooves

Their feet
Heavy,
Bruised
Hide in the rhythms
No counts left over
None wanting

A singer
Birds in his
      throat
Wears no white tie
Does not wipe life
      clean
Before swallowing
      wine

The guitarist
Hands like oil
Drips cigarette ash
      on his guitar
Plays in his
      shroud

~

Half-done, raw
The music escapes
Before it is
            ready

A clock ticks zero
You and I, we see
        only parts
And imagine the whole

Mario: Guitarist

Pineapple on a window sill
In the early a. m. of Spain.
(Sun by Matisse).

I hear the shimmer of trills,
High grass, and river flowing with shawl fringe.

Water ripples through guitar strings,
Giving promises that God is a Lady
With a rose in her hair and perfume
   at her breasts.

Chenin: Singer

The coarse edge to his big voice.
The whole land, like moldy earth,
Held in his closed hands

(I taste Spain under my tongue)

His sound shapes itself around the words
And they fall away from inside, leaving
Empty, crying, spaces.

Lourdes: Dancer

Beyond her heels, the click of details:
Head, hands, eye, skirt, fan, shawl, shoulders,
                    hips
Ripple from her center, touch on each other,
                    never overlap

Or she pauses, holding stillness in her body.
Then bends low,
In a long curve, shawl outstretched behind her,
A great bird's wing slowly turns.

Flamenco Guitarist

Curve of the
     moon
Narrow neck lined
       with lights
Gritty sounds
Low behind our own

What are they
      becoming?

The guitarist sits
Between black doors
Hands rustling and
     rapid

What is he making?

One note ceases
As another becomes the
Lime cool
Sweet-sour jazz of
       flamenco

Head bent over the
     strings
He follows
A river just being
   born.

Cante Jondo

When the Gypsies had
        no home on earth
Still they sang
Their wails wandering
        the night

Aiii...
What did you do today?
I buried my grandfather
But we couldn't stop
        long enough
To leave a marker.

Flicking rhythms off
        their tongues
They let out the bats
        and owls
Of sorrow

Aiii...
You came to my
        bedside
But didn't take me.
Death, when you left
I cried.

Fearing to be found out
Hiding
Whether necessary
    or not
They told their story

Aiii...
This morning
I married the woman
    I love
But the Guardias *are*
    after me
With knives in their
    hearts.

Black leaves lit
                by sunlight
Birds with only one day
                to live
Still the Gypsies sang

Aiii...
When daylight comes
My grief begins to
                grow
Only darkest night
Comforts my soul.

Alegrías

The night
Swallowed in wine
Until *no more*
Juanito still sitting
        in a low
            sunken sofa
His oily tawny face
            melancholy
Could purse his lips
Throw back his head
And sing such joy
As it hurt to hear:

Tiri tiri ti
Tran tran tran...

Scat singer
Sly sounds
Bird phrases:

Trabili tran
Traqui tran tran tran...

Wrapped in worries
No child of nature
Yet he sang the
        Alegrías:

Oli oli que oli oli
     que oli...

~

How did he do what
I never felt before?

Country Flamenco

Amid a colliding landscape strewn
      with boulders
And the molding ruins of an
      old castle
In a white town of no name
Life leans on a stick
To watch a dog cross the
      street

In dark doorways
Old women all in black
Crochet pale string
While other women steer
      goats
Down narrow channels
Between the rows of
      houses

In a patio
An old man in a straight-back
      chair
Sings the crusty sound of
      country flamenco
From deep down in the pocket
      of his throat:

Man goes through his days
like a stone through the air,
waiting to fall.

His songs stop time
Evoke the slender moon
      of loss:
His small white town is
      slowly disappearing.

Los Ultimos

The elder Gypsy flamencos are called <u>Los Ultimos</u>, *The Best.*

They speed beyond my control
This rowdy storming bunch
These Gypsies:

Tía Anica
Knees bent as an old
      sailor
Dances and dishes out
Little obscenities with
      her hands

Tío Tomás sits
Bangs his cane
Pulls the *cante jondo*
Through his warped
      throat

Old Farruco dances his
      big belly
Flipping it side to side
Every step

Fernanda
String bean body
Jackal's face
Weeps her reluctant
      song

Crazy-eyed Dieguito
Having lost his moon
Bends over his guitar
Listening to his only
      love

~

I'll tell you—sometimes
I groan to break away
Say, *enough*
But I always come back
To their mystery

But I ask you, Doloré
What mystery?
We live we sing
And whatever comes—
         comes
There is no beginning
You see, Doloré?

Deception

Ana Maria speaks: *Since my grandma died I keep hearing her call my name. My Aunt Pastora says I should answer her.*

~

Magdalena in her grave heard the forces of nature discussing her fate. She heard the earth grinding as it turned on its axis, the tug and pull of the other planets. She heard seeds popping open underground, she heard the worms starting to scrape and chew on her flesh.

Death was not, as she had expected, quiet. But it was lonely. None of her clan who had already gone to Glory could talk to her, nor she to them.

Her only recourse was the name of her little nine year old granddaughter, Ana Maria. She repeated it over and over.

She was repeating it still when she felt herself suddenly lifted aloft on a bed of light and carried off to Glory.

~

Magdalena spent most of her time in Glory sitting on an alabaster bench watching the celestial hierarchals wheel in flight around a central light more brilliant than a hundred suns.

Magdalena should have been ecstatic. But the Seraphim with their six wings constantly beating made her nervous. The Thrones with their bodies of fire frightened her. But the worst by far were the Cherubim: with their forty sets of eyes Magdalena felt she was being watched all the time.

111

Nor did she enjoy the other glories of Glory. The Elysian Fields were boring—nothing ever withered, dried up, or died. There was never a bug, a slug, or a snail. Nor did she like her own life—nothing to plan for, nothing to gain, and nothing to lose.

In short, Magdalena was miserable in Glory.

She wanted to discuss her problem with a celestial. It was not, however, an easy thing to bring one of them down to her level. It was finally an angel, of the 399,000 hierarchals, the very lowest order, that at last left off its rapturous flight long enough to settle on the alabaster bench with Magdalena and listen to her.

Not that Magdalena minded talking to only an angel. But even talking to a lowly angel had its protocols. Angels speak only in epiphanies, one-word epiphanies. Out of that one word Magdalena would be obliged to distill Divine Meaning.

Seated opposite the angel, Magdalena phrased her problem simply: she took no joy, no glory, in Glory.

Magdalena did not ask the angel to solve her problem. She knew enough to know that angels do not do the dirty work for humans. They give direction, subtle proddings, advice.

The angel listened, her small body glistening and shimmering, the feathers of her large, white wings riffling from the breezes of the other flying celestials. Then, putting a finger to her lips, tremulous with the excitement of her inspiration, she uttered one word: *Deception.*

Magdalena, alone again on the alabaster bench, pondered the angel's word. Deception was as natural to Magdalena as breathing. Among other things, she had stolen money from her clan, lied to her Father Confessor, and refused her son Aurelio forgiveness, even after he cut off his own finger for her.

Now it seemed to Magdalena that the angel was encouraging her to use deception to solve her dilemma.

Magdalena had no difficulty with that. Furthermore, she knew exactly what she wanted: it would be Glory enough for her to live and see the world again as a child. The only problem, of course, was that as an incorporeal, she would require someone else's body to do it.

Magdalena chose to return to earthly life as Ana Maria.

~

Ana Maria, her eyes wide open, had lain in her bed two days—not eating and not speaking. The third day, her Aunt Pastora, alarmed, called in the *bruja*.

The lumpy, dumpy *bruja*, her face lined like a rutted road, arrived with her basket of amulets, talismans, herbs, roots, animal entrails, and cantharides. She placed a powder made from the teeth of a white dog on Ana Maria's tongue. She rubbed her temples with the brains of a magpie. She tied red string around Ana Maria's wrists. She spat on her forehead. Nothing brought Ana Maria around.

Finally the old *bruja* sat back in her chair, looked up at Pastora and said she feared the worst. She asked Pastora to bring a dishpan of water in which she placed two straws. When one of them sank to the bottom of the pan, the *bruja* sighed heavily and nodded her head. She knew: Ana Maria was 'possessed.'

~

As quiescent as Ana Maria may have seemed, however, to the *bruja* and Pastora, inside her there was a battle raging, a noisy battle with Magdalena who, sometimes moaning and sometimes wailing, called to Ana Maria from across the bottomless abyss of death, begging and pleading that Ana Maria let her in.

But Ana Maria, who had always wanted to please her grandma, knew that this time she must not. With a will as strong as Magdalena's, she said *no*.

Then Magdalena changed her approach. Her voice became cooing, cloying. She reminded Ana Maria of all she had learned from her. Because of her, Ana Maria could make flowers bloom out of season. She could move dark clouds across the sky. Rats and mice would leave the caves simply because she asked them. "Ana Maria," Magdalena cajoled, "haven't you missed me, child? Just think, child, we would be together again, you and me. All you have to do, Ana, is let me in, let me share in your life."

But Ana Maria, doubting her grandma for the first time, knew she didn't want to share in Ana Maria's life—she wanted to *become* Ana Maria. "No, Grandma, no," Ana Maria sobbed, "I don't want you anymore!"

Magdalena was stunned. She had expected resistance from Ana Maria but not rejection. Like a sea anemone closing in on itself, Magdalena retreated, abashed.

Still, Ana Maria continued to be possessed.

~

The *bruja* sat for a long time looking at the straw at the bottom of the dishpan of water. Finally she spoke "Who was the last to die in your clan?" she asked Pastora.

When Pastora replied, "Magdalena," the *bruja* knew who was possessing Ana Maria.

Magdalena's clan, angry at her for stealing money, had not attended her funeral, and especially, they had not held a *juerga* for her. Her clan had always seen the dying off with a *juerga,* a flamenco party with everyone singing and dancing, eating and drinking. Why mourn for one who isn't dead yet?

For Ana Maria to be 'un-possessed,' the *bruja* said Magdalena's funeral rites would have to reenacted.

So Ana Maria's room was cleared and, in the middle of it, Ana Maria was laid out on a table.

Pastora, running up and down the streets of her barrio in her best dress, asked every Gypsy to the funeral. No one questioned.

Bringing wine, sausages, bread and extra chairs, the Gypsies danced and sang all night, ate and drank until dawn. Then Pastora folded Ana Maria's arms on her chest and made the sign of the cross over her. And the *bruja,* bathing her in salt water and dressing her in five blouses, five petticoats and five skirts, pronounced her *dead* and ready to be buried.

The Gypsies sobbed; they wept, they screamed, they hollered— until noon when they picked up their chairs and went home.

They had scarcely left when Ana Maria, speaking for the first time in three days, told Pastora she was hungry.

Pastora was delighted. But the *bruja,* attributing Ana Maria's return to her own cleverness, asked double her fee. Pastora's husband Pepino, enraged, said the whole thing was nonsense. Any idiot could see that Ana Maria woke up from all the noise.

~

Magdalena, pacing back and forth in the Elysian Fields, ranted and raved to herself: *Ana Maria is spoiled, ungrateful, and selfish.*

It was several days—earth time—before she began to take a certain pride in Ana Maria's strength. After all, wasn't Ana Maria who she was because of Magdalena? And several days after that before Magdalena called to the angel again and asked if she had another Word for her.

Sitting on the alabaster bench and listening to Magdalena, the angel's pale face grew even paler as Magdalena told her what she had attempted to do. Then the angel, pondering, one dimpled finger over her lips, finally spoke. *Self,* the angel said, and quickly left.

Magdalena, putting the words *Self* and *Deception* together, did not like it. Even if she admitted, or if she denied, she was self-deceiving, she could still be deceiving herself, couldn't she? There was no knowing the truth. Except for one thing: Magdalena knew she was miserable in Glory. Or, she wondered, *was* she in Glory?

Magdalena had prided herself on bypassing Purgatory. But a cold chill cut through her: if indeed she was in Purgatory and not in Glory, she did not know it. And because she was self-deceiving, she might wander the mazes of Purgatory—or was it Glory?—forever, never knowing, never finding a way out, and always miserable.

Epilogue

Ana Maria speaks: *Aunt Pastora and I put all my furniture back in my room after everyone left. That's when I found my mirror, the one my grandma gave me for my last birthday. It was smashed in a hundred pieces. I know my grandma did it. She is very mad at me. Aunt Pastora said I shouldn't hate my grandma for what she tried to do. Maybe she's right. But I will never put flowers on my grandma's grave again.*

In Remembrance
L.A.D.
(1929-1991)

It wasn't night
Or afternoon
The air was pale
    yellow
It must have been
    morning

The flamenco singer
Sitting in a straight
    black chair
Her face
A fan of wrinkles

Having sung all night
Narrowed her voice
And broke open the
    dawn

I could speak
    then
Tell you about
The tall gentle-eyed
    man
Who had held my flesh
Shed his tears with
    mine
Breathed into the palm
    of my hand

Tell you
He has taken
The long train
Across the last
    bridge

But in my memory
He is young again
He laughs and smiles
      again
While I turn only
      half my face
To the world.

Author's Note

The expression, *"Aiii...,"* half-spoken, half-sung, has no literal translation. It conveys the emotional quality and anguish of the deep songs—the laments—of the *cante jondo* repertoire and the intense religious conviction of the *saetas*. Its origin is believed to be the early morning call to prayer of the Moslem religion.

Acknowledgments

There are many people I wish to thank for their encouragement and support. I begin with the late Rosalie Moore—teacher, friend, and mentor—and Evelyn Belvin and Kathleen Burgy, all of whom I miss and from whom I learned so much. There are other California friends, among them Barbara Brauer and Jean Pumphrey, who continue to offer me insight and inspiration. I met the late Julian Battaile through Mary and Ed Brubaker. Julian, opening his home every week to writers, introduced me to many Oregon writers. My current writing group, both friends and critics, are Fanda Bender, Gloria Boyd, Melissa Brown, Patricia Florin, Ellen Gardner, Addie Greene, Deborah Rothschild, and Dorothy Vogel. Marilyn Joy and Sonja Ferrera of the group have since left Oregon and are missed.

I also wish to thank Roberta Kent, retired literary agent, for her continuing advice, support, and encouragement. And special thanks go to Nancy Parker, my editor, publisher and the designer of this book.

About the Author

Dolores de Leon performed as a ballet dancer, modern dancer, and flamenco dancer in Los Angeles, San Francisco, New York, and Spain. She led and choreographed her own modern dance and flamenco companies in San Francisco. One of her ballets remains among the permanent repertoire of the Oakland Ballet Company. She taught modern dance at Dominican University in San Rafael, California.

As a writer, her short stories reflecting the lifesyle, belief systems, and traditions of the Gypsies of southern Spain have been published in the following literary journals: *Amoskeag, Arnazella, Convululus, Left Curve, The Madison Review, RiversEdge, Thereby Hangs a Tale,* and *Zahir.*

She served as an executive member of the Marin Poetry Center in San Rafael and a member of the Board of Directors of Intersection Art Center in San Francisco.

She now resides in southern Oregon.

The author dancing in a cramped studio in Sevilla.

www.ingramcontent.com/pod-product-compliance
Lightning Source LLC
Chambersburg PA
CBHW020629250626
47154CB00004B/1733